»What happens in the City has never affected us more.«

Philip Coggan, ›The Money Machine. How the City Works‹

TAMO GENGEL

HOW PEOPLE IN ENGLAND FEEL ABOUT LONDON AS FINANCIAL CENTRE

DIFFERENT VOICES ABOUT THE CITY

This travel book is the result of a project sponsored by a scholarship of ZIS, Schule Schloss Salem [www.zis-reisen.de/index-en.html]; it was also supported by the United Nations Educational, Scientific and Cultural Organization

Please note: the comments from my interview partners reflect their own views and not the views of any specific company! I also had to keep some of my interviewees anonymous or change their names at their request.

© 2013 Tamo Gengel, Karlsruhe

tamogengel@yahoo.de

manufactured and published by:

BoD-Books on Demand, Norderstedt, Germany
ISBN 9783732235445

Contents

My first impressions..7

»London is a playground for rich people«....17

The London Interviews...................................30

Why London works as a financial centre......96

Three words depicting London's
financial centre..99

London without its financial industry?.......103

What will change?..112

Non-profit-organisations at London's
financial districts..119

What I noticed...124

What I learned from London........................141

A few numbers about my project.................149

The most memorable statements..................156

What I found interesting. Media list............160

Thank you! Acknowledgements....................164

First impressions

Getting off the bus in London I spot 33 cash machines from the Bank of America right up to the Zurich Invest Bank lined up next to each other, flashing like a chain of pearls. Immediately someone offers me 17,000 toxic Greek bonds, a banker right next to him throws his £500,000 cash-received bonus triumphantly into London's smog-soaked air. While in the background three citizens with Guy-Fawkes-masks start smashing the cash machines with their baseball bats into ten thousand pieces …

Did this really just happen? Does the world's biggest financial centre confront a visitor at first sight with these prejudices? Well, stepping off that bus into London's unclouded sun I indeed spotted a dozen cash machines from widely different banks at first glance.

Yet I don't think this is to be associated with the size of the local financial centre[1]. This is due to the overabundant population of London: the city must provide a tight net of functioning infrastructure and money supply facilities and so forth for about 10 million people in its greater region.

So how does the financial centre influence London? What do the City's business people think about their finance centre, the biggest on earth[2]? What attitudes lie behind their opinions? What does the opposing party, Occupy, have to say against the system?

---

[1] About 600.000 people of London's 8 million inhabitants work in the financial sector, according to the official British graduate-counselling.
[http://www.prospects.ac.uk/accountancy_banking_and_finance_sector_overview.htm]
[2] According to the Global Financial Centres Index 2012

I turned 18 a few days before my trip to Great Britain's capital, now I want to explore the financial centre from the viewpoint of a young man and answer these questions in the City itself.

I arrive at Victoria Station in the middle of peak time. Which way is the fastest now to get to the heart of the financial centre, the City of London? Obviously other folk have answered that question the same way I did: taking Central Line during rush hour, you'll see suits galore and a lot of people with briefcases and laptops. Central Line stops at a station called ›Bank‹; quite telling about what one can perceive at first glance of London's mighty finance industry: business people in packs use the elaborate traffic system London built up for them.

Here's a typical neon advertisement for the ›Bank‹-station:

An Online-Broker offers his small spread; the spread being the difference between the ask and the bid price of an investment product. The smaller the spread, the better.

Sign in a DLR train: ›Train is for Bank.‹

Besides the Tube as a transport facility, London has taxis, Docklands Light Railway DLR, double-decker buses or rentable bicycles with a big Barclays-logo on it. Tourists prefer the garish red double-decker buses; but most popular is the Tube, even for the finance business people. »The Tube now carries more than a billion people a year« – this advertisement from the London Underground speaks for itself.

Single trips with the Tube can cost you dear; the most favourable offer is the Oyster Card. This card calculates the cheapest way to get to your destination. Automated services like these track you step by step: they ensure quick fluid manoeuvres, specifically useful for finance women and men …

An overcrowded Tube you'll find only during peak times between 8-9 a.m. and 5-7 p.m. To prevent traffic jams, the traffic authorities keep rebuilding some selected stations. »The Tube is being upgraded to keep

London moving« – one more advertisement from the London Underground.

To prevent jams, there are rules in London's traffic system, like on escalators: »stand right, walk left!,« which some ignorant tourists don't follow, and for this hampering of the seamless flow of the masses they sometimes get their heads bitten off by annoyed residents used to move smoothly and uninterruptedly …

Why is all that important when looking at a finance centre? I first noticed the modern infrastructure necessary to make frictionless actions possible for the Londoners. It's the infrastructures that set the imperatively essential frame, in which a finance centre might flourish.

But I only perceived the tremendous extent of London's infrastructures only bit by bit, in details. And my impression, honestly? Many finance business people take it for granted or are not aware of this infrastructure supporting them. Well, they don't have to be, it's automated, right? There must be somebody in the City Hall who has keen eyes on the mighty correlation between business and local facilities[3].

So you will take the Central Line – how symbolical – to the finance centre. When I first got to the City – that's how Londoners call the financial district –, I quickly realise: it is way too big to be overlooked on a one time visit.

I deliberately went there during the morning peak to experience the rush hour. Unique experience for a newcomer! Hundreds of business men here and there and every… But here you will not find another Shibuya, the largest crossroad of the world in Tokyo, as there is no such big a central place where all

---

[3] Big generators enforcing the London financial economic miracle should be lawmakers, lobbyists, agents of bank associations …

the major thoroughfares merge, where hundreds of people will cross the central downtown place at once.

No, the financial institutions are spread throughout half of London. There are three major centres: The City, Canary Wharf, and Mayfair. ›The City‹, that is downtown London, does not by all means appear to be crammed full of banks, as some people might imagine; you will rather find it a place for insurance companies and investment funds. Canary Wharf, located in the southeast of London, is known for its multi-story high rise buildings and represents the actual banking district. Mayfair became a well-liked area for hedge funds, financial consultants or private banking services. Mayfair is located in the West of London and counts as a richer area. Thus wealthy fund managers have their workplace almost right in front of their alarmed front doors. And it's only a short commute for those who live in Chelsea or Notting Hill.

Rush hour in the middle of the City

Almost everyone around me in the City seems tremendously busy, with their smartphones pressed to their ears and the free [!] City A.M. finance-newspaper or a briefcase tucked under their left arm.

One of my interview partners, Bertrand Beghin, describes London's office towers as anthills, in which the employees swarm around like ants in teams and work together. At 9:15 a.m. most of the Cityboys are at their desks in the office towers, many will still be there after 8 p.m.

Business style men with suits in the City; in the background the Bank of England with advertisement banners for the Olympics

»London is a playground for rich people«

»There are the wealthiest people in London,« a senior asset management executive told me. The expensive restaurants and bars, the exclusive events, the big glass facades of the finance buildings, maybe some pretty women, but pretty sure the expensive British cars like Bentleys or Aston Martins and the biggest financial centre in front of the front door: that makes London a »playground« for rich people like Russian oil billionaires or hedge fund managers, he explained.

Hedge funds are speculative investment funds as they often operate with sophisticated techniques. That is to say: in what financial products exactly the responsible manager invests the money, can be hard to figure out; and he will hardly reveal his operating strategy to a stranger. To dodge constricting laws and to save money, the hedge fund managers use several smart tricks, which makes hedge funds risky. »They are usually registered in an offshore haven like the Cayman Islands to give them tax privileges … but this also means they are very lightly regulated.«[4]

Here money is made during daytime and spent in the evening. For instance, one of my hosts, Mr Scooter, would leave his office earlier as his boss went to yoga with a client for the evening.

---

[4] »The Money Machine. How the City Works«; Philip Coggan, p. 84

A limousine at Canary Wharf by night

»The client is the king,« he will be invited to all kinds of events, like golf, to a pub or on a nightclub side trip. Obviously, the Olympics came in useful for everyone [the games took place in London as the only city for the third time]. Matthew, an intern at a sovereign wealth fund, told me, all his colleagues went to the Olympics with their clients, except himself. He had to spend half the night at the office, as »interns are welcomed to overstrain themselves.« Many City employees spoke of

15 hour-workdays; leaving home at 8 a.m. and being home at 12 p.m. Otto Dixx, an investment professional of a real-estate fund, had to shift our meeting three times as he »gets killed at the moment in the office,« he wrote to me, »in a metaphorical sense, of course …«

»It's important to know the client, he should feel like you're his friend,« said Tobias, an asset manager of a fund at Lloyd's Building. »The client should feel: we are in the same boat, and his money is safe at your fund. Without clients, you definitely do not survive at the world's biggest finance centre.« No clients, no money.

The finance sector belongs to the service sector, »something a fund manager must never forget,« emphasized a senior asset management executive. Investment managers offer a service which only can operate with investors, respectively clients. »It is not your own money that you manage, but your client's money.«

It became a popular sport to criticise the salaries of top bankers or hedge fund managers. »Quite a few of these clowns earn more in a week than a teacher in a year …«[5] If someone is buying a 20 million apartment at west end or outbidding a Russian billionaire at a Sotheby's auction, the chances are it is an hedge fund or private equity titan.

James Almighty is one of these. He mentioned an unexpected but interesting reason for the size of the salaries. He began with »there is one thing or one reason that answers the question« and then he added: »The finance business is the only industry with scale ability!«

Let's say a fund manager starts with managing £5 million. He succeeds, so other investors also invest their money in his fund. Eventually he manages £500 million. The interesting

---

[5] »Cityboy. Beer and Loathing in the Square Mile«; Geraint Anderson; p. 139

thing however is: he does not necessarily have to hire more people in order to manage these assets [he does not even have to change strategies or even the size of his office].

That is what Mr Almighty points out: the volume he controls increases, but not mandatorily the numbers of employees. For the bank account it is indifferent, whether there are £100.000 standing or £500.000.000 – a bank account bears further digits before the decimal point trouble-free. But the greater the fund volume, the higher the salary because of the success fee [which of course also depends on the returns], though he does the same job.

This unlimited scale ability definitely differs in other industries, for example the car industry. More orders amount inescapably in more material and more employees – with roughly the same wages for every worker …

I asked one interviewee in a high position, how many people work at his firm. He answered: »On a good day – about 80%!« Despite a 70-80 hour workweek, he had a witty remark in stock for every question[6]! Or vice versa: can only someone with humour master such a focussing mental performance each day? Maybe that's the reason why ›Cityboy‹ Geraint Anderson thinks, the most important things in the City were parties where one can swap information and absorb the pressure with casual banter.

Regarded by the inhabitants lacking big money, London seems nearly unpayable. Rental prices are incredibly high: you have to pay £1700 for a 46 m² one-room flat in Central London, £1000 for the same size in Brixton. Compared to Germany: in Cologne you pay £400 for a 50 m² apartment. The Tube ticket for £1200 for one year is unaffordable for quite some people; eating out might soon become tough for average earners, the price for a little ›baguette to-go‹ is at £5; in Berlin

---

[6] It might be a dozen coworkers.

you would get 2 or 3 baguettes for this price.

One waitress of a very popular global coffee company even accounted her own products as overpriced, unofficially speaking. But two-thirds of her customers are business people, who meet in these coffee houses with their clients. »They often talk about business, they would not mind the prices.«

Similar the opinions of the passers-by I surveyed. London booms, you'll pay a high ›staying-here-fee‹ to experience an impressive city which you can't entirely make use of, as many things are unaffordable. A cinema ticket in London's inner city may cost north of £20, which might take a small family to the screen in Germany. So that is the first effect of the financial centre on the rest of London town: where some people earn big money, prices are rising for all other people, too.

However, the financial centre has positive side effects for London. If the finance industry boosts, the entertainment and art branch in London get spurred. Marta, from an organisation for business consultants, confirms: »The financial sector here creates job opportunities,«, and adds: »but the price range stays up – a bad aspect for people not working in finance business.«

9 out of 10 interviewees addressed this topic, the high price level. Shakespeare's advice »put money in thy purse«[7] obviously still holds, if you intend to travel to Great Britain's capital. Brett Scott, a two year worker as a derivates broker in the City and now blogging about his explorations on the financial system[8], reinforced that the high price level substantially affects other industries. »London as a financial centre impacts the entire world,«

---

[7] ›Othello‹ 1,3

[8] http://suitpossum.blogspot.de/ [In the meantime, Brett is funding a school for monetary education.]

was one of his statements.[9]

With all its terrific and fantastic City-buildings, London attracts more than 30 million tourists from all parts of the earth in one year. ›The Gherkin‹, designed by Norman Foster, who also built the Commerzbank Tower in Frankfurt and the Shanghai-Bank high-rise in Hong Kong, is a building in the middle of the financial centre's heart in London.

---

[9] E.g., the price for wheat more than doubled in 2010, from $150 per ton to $370, through speculators at the commodities market. In 2011, people in Algeria protested against a sudden 30% price increase on their daily bread; yet ›bread riots‹ have been epidemic in Egypt, Tunisia, Haiti, Bangladesh ever since stock adventurers drove up prices, thousands got killed, 260.000 starved from the end of 2010 and April 2012 in Somalia only. To this I heard from several people, staple food should maybe be excluded from uncompromising speculation.

Architecturally, the ›City‹ sets European standards also with the just accomplished skyscraper ›The Shard‹ by Renzo Piano [he also designed the Centre Pompidou in Paris]. With the Shards 310 m height, London has the continent's highest building [if you don't class Moscow amongst Europe].

And the construction of prestige buildings goes on; you will spot many construction zones and big cranes.

In 2014, for instance, the Leadenhall Building will be on view directly between Lloyd's and The Gherkin.

The London Interviews

I really would have liked to show pictures of my interview partners right here. None of them, however, would agree to recording: no sound recording, no photographs – no names at all … Neither bankers, nor Occupy-supporters: no single one of them. This precise denial surprised me. Controversial positions, evidently. Rule #1, therefore: no names! I had to change them.

But after all, it's the content of the interviews that counts. Here are some excerpts; all of them were taking place in August and September 2012.

Tobias, asset-manager, dialogue in a bar next to the Lloyd's Building

- What would London represent without its financial centre?

Without the financial centre, the city itself would be poorer, much poorer. In the 1980s, London suffered from its dwindling population.[10] Since then, about 1.5 million new inhabitants accrued. London mainly grew in consequence of the expansion of the former port, Isle of Dogs, into the high-rise complex Canary Wharf. New employment developed, making the city richer in every way. The financial industry had been the motor of urban development for the last 30 years.

- What has been your most remarkable or striking day in the city?

About 10 years ago, when I was still a broker, one Monday morning a representative of a company came to me telling how strong his company was. He ushered me to buy shares of his business company by all means. Since I

---

[10] In 1940 there lived 9 million people in London, in 1980 just about 6,8 million.

was young and new to the business I trusted him and bought some shares the following Tuesday. On Friday, this company share lost 50% of its value. It turned out: the representative had been lying, he knew about the upcoming plunge. From this I learned: it's hard to trust people with money.

Also 9/11 was an extraordinary and dreadful day! After the crash in the WTC it only took 9 seconds and the market had lost a fifth of its value, 20%!

- What does your normal workday look like?
A normal day looks like this: at 6:30 I'm already at the office watching the news. Then I will call different clients talking about interesting investments. When the exchange market opens I will start trading. It pleases me that no day is like the other, since at the stock exchange the same thing never happens twice. The worst thing about my job is when you have to tell your customer you lost money …

▪ How do people change when they get rich?
Good question! Let me quote George Orwell:
»Rich people are like poor people with money.«

The illuminated Lloyd's Building at dawn

Lily Lapenna, CEO and founder of MyBnk

▪ What do you like about the City?
The buildings in the City of London are magnificent. Also, the group of office block build-

ings on the Isle of Dogs, Canary Wharf, is fantastic.

With more than 300,000 employees, the financial sector is one of the biggest in London. I appreciate the City for the economy itself, for the fact that so many are employed here. This creates prosperity for the city of London.

- What is it you dislike about the financial centre?

Banks commit a whole lot of real money to even very young traders to ›bet‹ or ›gamble‹ with, as they call it themselves. In the investment banking business many risky deals will breed the greed for money in the executives. And at one time they will totally blow it and gamble away such a big deal. Not only London, but sadly the whole world must assume the consequences, for the investment banking business is operating on a global platform.

- What is your personal professional aim?
It is my ambition to grant young people access to economic knowledge and insight. This will improve the living quality of a great many.

Reuters Building, displaying the share prices; in Canary Wharf

I addressed a banker in the open street for an interview; he asked me whether we could get it done while walking since he was in a hurry. He wore a suit, looked like a Cityboy and was approximately 30 years young.

- What is money? Do you like money?

If it comes down to money, to me this always means: making money. And by making money you better be able to calculate the risk. Business is about control. Doing deals it pays to control the risk and to reduce it at best.

- What kind of work would you detest, even at the same salary?

Mmh, do you see him? [He points at a building labourer in a road construction zone.] This kind of work. Even at better wages …

- What pleases you about London's financial centre?

Best about the finance centre here I favour the whole network and the functioning system. Here you can call anybody you need and he'll be there. No matter if it's the analyst of Goldman Sachs, the trader from Citigroup or your lawyer.

- What is your personal goal?
My personal goal is to open my own hedge fund together with my friends and to successfully manage it. then we were more independent from our employer, which would make all things easier.

With its 236 m height the Canada Square Building on Canary Wharf is the second tallest building in London, following »The Shard«

David Dewhurst, Occupy-activist

- What do you think of London's centre of finance in general?

In my opinion it is a disappointment. It is helping the economy, but it destroys more than it helps. The persons responsible for the risky deals lost all real sense of what money is.

- What influence does the City have on London town?

It pumps a lot of money into the capital. Consequently, the price level is enormously high compared to other large European cities. You can hardly afford a cup of coffee.

- Don't you like money?

Yes, sure I do! But not as much as to screw my own customers.

- Why do, from your point of view, bankers mostly wear suits?

Suits radiate respectability. And they make the men wearing them prouder than they are, which actually is ridiculous.

- Do you envy the finance businessmen?
I wouldn't mind having a lot of money! But many of the finance tradespeople live a strenuous, yet dull life. I'm glad not to be one of them.

An occupy-sticker saying ›liberation-occupy‹, stuck on a rented bicycle above the company logo of Barclays

Mike Mompi, head of innovation with the non-profit organisation »MyBnk«

- What does money mean to you? Do you like money?
Money is omnipresent; it doesn't have a real value. And only a small part of humanity

commands a great deal of money. An interesting fact: 1 percent of the population owns 99 percent of all global capital. Thus the ›remnant‹ 99 percent own merely one percent! We ought to introduce our children at an early age to monetary policy. Personally, I like the principle of ›shared-value-concept‹ which assists the economy in a sustainable not at all short-sighted way.[11]

- Are you dissatisfied with anything concerning the City?

There are a number of things! First of all I am dissatisfied with the narrow perspective people in the financial industry gain. I have some friends who earn half a million pounds per annum at the age of just about 25 years.

---

[11] The shared-value-concept raises the competitive strength of a company and at once improves the conditions of the community in which it works, financially and socially.

This ruins their sense of reality, their view of money and of life.

Time is my second objection. All things go so fast here and they never stop. The schedule is so busy that you have to tell your friends »I will have thirty minutes in two weeks' time to meet you.« That's simply absurd!

▪ What is your personal goal?
I want to create solutions that, in the process of creating, enlighten the financial centre of the self interest it has in creating shared value across all of the society.

In the inner courtyard, there are the offices of MyBnk

Bertrand Beghin, Co-Founder of Numbers4Good and Ex-banker

▪ What makes London special as financial centre?

London's famous role is its status as a one of the main financial centre in the world, especially as a leader of the foreign exchange trading. A lot of money goes through London. Also the time zones are important as London covers Wall Street and Asia for financial services. The US is more controlled.

▪ Do finance people take pride in their image?

Good question! First, I think people don't show someone, who dresses badly, that much respect as they do for people with suits. Finance people look more serious if they dress like that. But it also can be deceiving. And second, it is a bit of a psychological thing: you don't have to think about what you are going to wear today at work. So it is easier just to pick a suit and it fits with everybody else in this industry.

■ What is your goal? Or what would be the Jackpot for you?
I want to establish and develop sustainability within the finance industry. The last crises showed how vulnerable this sector can be if something goes in the wrong way.

I personally took a leap from ›mainstream finance‹ to the finance business with an social background and focus, hence I founded Numbers4Good.

Offices at night, close to the Bank of England

Brett Scott, blogger, ex-broker

■ What makes London a unique financial location?

London is one of the few truly international financial centers. It spans three time zones – Asia and Australia in the morning, Europe, Middle East and Africa during the day, and the Americas at night. New York is also a huge financial centre but it is more focused on the domestic US economy; London is focused on investments outside of the UK. London is also at the centre of a global network of tax havens[12] – places like the Cayman Islands host loads of hedge funds and other investment vehicles that funnel business back to the

---

[12] Of the 25 leading hedge fund domiciles 10 are either directly administered by the British Crown or members of the Commonwealth; [the number 1, Cayman Island, is a British colony; Guernsey, Jersey, Isle of Man, British Virgin Islands, Gibraltar etc. follow].

City. In case the London administrators raised taxes, many financial services and banks would leave the city, they say. In my opinion, this is bullshit! First of all, London would never do that, and secondly, London still would be the first place of all financial locations.

- Is there anything you dislike about the City?
There are many negative problems associated with the financial sector, but at a human level it's problematic that so many young people get drawn into it – they may be enticed by the promise of high pay, or they may go in simply because their friends do it, but either way, a lot of them get trapped in there. The financial sector can be interesting, but if all your top graduates are being drawn into an industry that doesn't produce anything in particular: it's not a good thing. Young professionals waste their lives in order to sometime later make a lot of money. For this, they attended

colleges like Oxford and Cambridge. These two universities direct students into four different professional areas: 1. investment banking; 2. accounting and bookkeeping; 3. law; 4. business consultancy.

So, lots of graduates who could be building interesting new renewable energy systems that have real long-term benefits for the world are rather spending their time designing pointless algorithms to help a hedge fund execute an order three milliseconds faster. A lot of time spent in the financial business is useless time. For example, I spent two years of my life as derivative broker and now I am obviously the only expert on one sort of insignificant derivative that no one uses right now.

▪ How did you end up in the financial business?
I entered the sector as part of an anthropologically-inspired adventure to discover what was going on inside. I came from the left-wing

movements – most of whom are very against the financial sector – and I openly explored the sector to get a feel for the internal dynamics. A few of my friends and I were going to break into the system of a certain bank. For this, we had to act as though we were going to seriously apply for a job, in order to gain insight into the setting of their system. In reality I never wanted to have the job I was applying for. Surprisingly, however, I was accepted! So I thought: »Come on, give it at least a try!« and started working. But I never intended to work there in the longer term.

I actually had a very interesting time, and made many good friends within the sector, who are still my friends. Now I try to help bridge the gap between campaign groups and the financial sector.

- Why is the number of women so small in the financial sector?

The leadership positions in the banking industry are still dominated by old white men who rose up the ranks back in the 1970s when the sector was much less open or meritocratic. This applies to 95% of the banks or other financial services here in London.

The number of women is comparatively low because they were only encouraged or allowed access into the sector much later than men, but the number of women has increased a lot over the years, largely because they're often better at the job than men and are less prone to suffering from over-inflated egos.

Typical street scenery between the Lloyd's and the Willis Building.

A senior asset management executive of a mutual fund company

- What does money mean to you? Do you like money?

It is important that you fully appreciate when working for a financial institution that you are responsible for someone else's money. As a reliable financial advisor I realise that clients have placed a lot of trust in me and my company – this should not be taken for granted. So money is quite real for me and not something to play with. As a fund manager you have got to fulfil your fiduciary obligations and augment your customers' money. It is a factor that a lot of managers forget: it's not their own money.

- What does a fund manager have to be good at? Which quality is fundamental?

A fund manager has to possess a notably coherent view of the world. That's what makes him or her a good manager. Then their decisions can come out advantageously compared with others.

- What is special about the City?
Good question. London comprehends better than other cities how the financial service business works. I don't want to spell it out exactly; but financial service firms are better supported here than elsewhere ...[13]

- What would London be without its centre of

---

[13] For UK-hedge funds applicable: COLL, the Collective Investment Schemes Sourcebook, since 2007 legally binding for UK funds. Yet it's not only laws that help cities to function as a financial centre, but the lack of laws, the omission of administrative provisions. E.g., in London there is no legal norm concerning qualified investor scheme in terms of minimum investment, no legal norm concerning non-UCITS retail schemes [effective 2013].

finance?

Without its financial centre London would be less creative and less ground-breaking! Its prosperity also allows for other industries to grow, such as the fashion business, media and the creative arts. Without the City there wouldn't be many of the advantages London has to offer.

- What is your goal?

To ensure my clients' financial objectives are met. I always like to get positive feed-back from my customers, as to my investment company doing a good job. The trust placed in me by my clients to meet their objectives motivates me hugely. That's what I'm always working towards.

The Willis Building, next to Lloyd's

Ben France, trader of a British major bank

- What do you value about the financial centre of London?

Its diversity is a positive aspect. Right here, about 300.000 employees work in the same business, yet almost every one with a different assignment.

- Would you like to work somewhere else? Or why simply here in London?

Maybe in Asia. This region is booming and attracts more and more companies and financial services to work there. Asia has become a trend.

Office tower with different financial companies on Canary Wharf

Daniel Levitt, Occupy-protester

▪ What would you do, if on Trafalgar Square's forth, empty plinth there stood a banker's statue?
[Laughs and takes time to think.] We'd demonstrate, for sure!

▪ Are bankers' salaries fair in this place?
Bankers' salaries are far from fair here! They get money for burning money or destroying countries. That is incredible – but unfortunately true.

▪ Do you envy bankers?
Only for one thing: their boundless freedom after work!

Advertisement screen at Canary Wharf

James Almighty, credit analyst at a hedge fund

- What do you like about the City?

I have been working in London since 2001. The city has a high level of innovation, which appeals to me: as you have to deal with smart people only and everyone has a common goal. Next to my hedge fund business I operate in microeconomics. I have been investing into this start-up [he points at my water bottle, displaying ›CleanWater‹ on the label]. This way I'm also supporting young entrepreneurs.

- Which influence does the financial centre have on the rest of the town?

In my opinion it is typically European to think of London only as a financial city. I think, New York or Singapore are much more focussed on the finance industry.

In Great Britain everyone will visit its capital London, people of all classes come here, because there aren't so many major cities on the island. Therefore, London isn't just focussed on finance business, not everyone is working for the financial industry.

In Northern America, however, some of the young workers go to Chicago, some to Atlanta, and for the entertainment industry they go to L.A. But the ones wishing to work in the financial sector primarily go to New York.

- What kind of superpower would you like to possess?

I would like to be able to predict the future. The future is sometimes better than we think.

- What was your most remarkable day in the City?

Each day in the City you may be right or wrong, the pendulum of success may swing back and forth. The most blatant day clearly was 9/11. We were just talking on the phone with colleagues from the 100th floor of the

WTC at that particular time. I don't want to go into that much further; I am sorry. [He looks aside for a while.]

- What is money? Do you like money?
Money is just a facility[14]. We save it for the future and sometimes get it back with an interest rate, and those who have produced it gain a bonus. To earn the money is one thing. Much more important is, however, what you do with it, what kind of strategy you have.

- Why is the percentage of female managers rather small in the financial business?
[He thinks a while.] It depends what kind of jobs you are talking about. No matter if male or female, both can be very well-trained and both will be in the run for the time-consuming positions.

---

[14] The word ›facility‹ is a bank-specific term denoting the possibility to draw on a short-run credit or to create a balance.

In reality, however, it is different. If a 25-year-old male is looking for a woman, will he first of all look at her asset and her money? Not really. A 25-year-old woman looking for a man: will she be looking first of all at his asset and his money? More than she should!

This somewhat demonstrates how different both genders may tick. Boys are more inclined to play games, for example to trade [he smiles]. At school it already becomes apparent what is reflected in the cliché: many say, boys are better at maths and girls are more into languages.

At Canary Wharf at night

Katherine from Chelsea, a pedestrian

- In your opinion, what impact does the financial centre have on the city?
Unfortunately, everything is incredibly expensive here …

- How do you treat your money? Do you trust the Cityboys?
My husband takes care of that [she laughs].

- Which three words best describe the City for you?
Fast, huge, and real. Real in a sense, that money is real and one really shouldn't play with it.

A German sports car in the City of London

Mr Retire, spokesman of a bank network

- Is there anything you don't like about the City?

I'd be silly to say »nothing«. Some people hate not to know what is going to happen. Actually, I like that! I'm definitely displeased with the long working hours, because you hardly ever see your family.

- What kind of person should not be working in the financial industry?

The ones without proven communicational skills. You ought to have a natural respectability and honesty. Some forget: the financial sector is a service sector offering the service to generate money for other people.

Illuminated glass fronts at Canary Wharf at night

Clive Menzies, presently Occupy-supporter, formerly broker and Cityboy

- Is there more illusion than reality in the financial business?

Definitely. The leverage effect of derivatives has a great impact on the real value of money. Markets are being more and more manipulated by computer trading programmes which destroy the usefulness of fundamental or technical analysis of prices. The market is becoming a casino in which price or index movements have no grounding in reality.

- What would London represent without the City?

London without the City would still be a vivid and dynamic metropolis. If the financial sector disappeared, other business and activity would take its place.

The ›2-More-London-Buildings‹ next to the City Hall, where the Mayor of London rules

> Julie Whittaker, communications adviser with Ashoka UK, an international non-profit organisation supporting young entrepreneurs

- What makes London unique as a financial location?

The City of London is less regulated than other financial centres like New York or Tokyo. London has been traditionally considered a city of commerce for a long time and continues to offer a competitive place of trading. The financial sector creates many jobs. About 350.000 employees are working there.

- What would London be without its financial centre?

It would be a totally different city. I would call it ›abandoned‹, as without the financial sector it would be much poorer – **given the tax paid by city institutions** –, and less developed.

- Why do so many people in the financial world wear suits, Miss Whittaker?

It's a tradition and rather oriented toward manliness. It is also part of the tradition and culture of this country, since suit, shirt and tie are ›very British‹. From a feminine point of view it also simplifies things, because you don't have to think about what you are going to wear today.

- Do the Cityboys' wages seem fair to you?

Yes and no. Outside of London many people are shocked when they hear about the high salaries. But I also appreciate that many of these jobs are highly risky and include very long days, which in a certain way needs to be rewarded.

The Bank of England building

Mark Cheng, director of Ashoka UK

■ Is there anything in the City you dislike?
In the financial business we had a number of crises and bubbles over the years, the worst of which of course is the current financial crisis which we are still in. These crises are driven in large part by the systemic and often perverse incentives that the City offers to its traders and money managers - massive bonuses if bets pay off, very little downside if things do not. Is there any surprise that this can foster a culture of greed and brash risk-taking?

The greed for money is too high and so are the wages. During my internship with Deutsche Bank I took part in a two-day conference in Barcelona. I found out that DB spent more than 200.000 € for drinks and concerts during this conference. This made me think.

■ Mr Cheng, what would London be like without its financial centre?

London is a powerful cultural centre for the arts and the music business; much more than a financial metropolis. There are so many people from different countries enriching London with diverse cultures. Although the financial centre drive certain forms of consumption and luxury at the high end of the market, London has a vibrancy that goes far beyond its role as a powerhouse of finance.

»The Shard« at night, worm's-eye view

Mike Group, warrant-trader at an American major bank

- What is it you like about the City?

I enjoy that those who gladly carry out their profession in the financial business assemble in this place: you are working together with smart people that all show an exciting background. Still all of them are broad-minded and open for other matters, not only being driven by the aim of becoming rich.

- And is there anything you dislike here?

The city of London is extremely expensive. From food to property. I am displeased with the great anonymity that exists in the City. There are too little conversations with an eye contact, almost everything works via e-mail or phone.

- Would you rather work somewhere else than London?

I feel comfortable in the city, and I like the structure and my employer's management.

- Do you think your job is secure?

Good question, Tamo! Of course, the risk to lose one's job is higher in investment banking than maybe in other branches. But if you are good at what you are doing, you do have a certain job security.

- Which three words best describe London as a financial location to you?

I'd say the City is impressive, intelligent, and innovative.

Office tower of Citigroup, Canary Wharf

> Marta West, executive manager at a business consultant organisation

- What kind of influence does the financial centre exert on London?

Evidently, the prices! But there are pros and cons. All together, it is great for the city since the financial centre represents some kind of developing area and helps cultivate London in a number of ways, for example in architecture, jobs or the security within the city, especially around the financial quarters … The drawback is the high price level, which strikes anyone not working in the financial business.

- What would London be without its City?

London would still remain an innovative location for uprising branches, even without its City. Not only London's financial industry is doing well on the race tracks, but also the arts and the music business. In case the financial sector collapsed, another of these huge industries would occupy this niche.

The City of London, seen from the Southern side of the Thames

Mr Anonymous, profession: banker at a major American bank. I addressed him in broad daylight during his presumed lunch break, asking him: »Sir, are you ready for five pounds, five questions?« He looks at me puzzled, grabs the 5 pounds from my fingers. It's a deal!

▪ Would you rather work anywhere else? Or does it simply have to be London?

I love this place! As you insinuate yourself: this is the centre; it's my personal honour to work here. You're in connection with many people, as London benefits from the different time zones. In my opinion, London is more focussed on finance than other cities are.

▪ Which three words describe the City of London best for you?

[He gets a call, answers and talks two minutes with his associate on the phone.] Who are you again? And what have we been talking about? Ah, yes: innovative, dynamic, and impressive: these are my three terms describing the City.

▪ What incident could lead to the worst disaster in the City of London?

[He thinks for a while, maybe lacking some concentration.] The rumour mill is buzzing due to statements from some big press agencies, TV, radio, papers or books. So, maybe even your book will lead to the greatest catastrophe in the City [laughs].

▪ What kind of work would you despise? Even at the same salary?!
[Laughs again] O boy, I put a lot of time and effort into becoming what I am right now. Well, I wouldn't want to be a trainee or an intern once again, since that virtually has been my worst time, spending most of my life in the office. Several times I had to stay the night in order to get my assignments done in time.

▪ Last question: What can I do for you to get my five pounds back?
[Laughs aloud.] Alright, just let me be Mr Anonymous in your book, ok?!

[He hands me back my money … Thank you, this is how I figured it out, Mr Anonymous[15].]

The Lloyd Building from inside

Dennis Lavine, employed at the M&A department of a major British bank

■ Are you happy to work here with regards to your job security?

---

[15] Interestingly, ›Anonymous‹ also stands for a movement critical towards capitalism.

[Laughs.] The security of one's job within the financial sector is – the same as in any other sector … You have to achieve a great performance, otherwise you might miss out.

At the moment I'm distinctly doing fine, because in my department we all get along and everyone is working as part of the team. But I'm aware, this could rapidly change.

▪ What could lead to a disaster in the City?
Rumours could cause great trouble for the financial centre of London. The media bloat a detail and cause ›global trouble‹. Then the public only gets the big news, the harmless detail remains unrevealed.

▪ What kind of secrets are hidden behind those glass fronts?
Manifold matters are completed behind these facades. Each single department has to cope with different duties. In a good company, all elements have to work together as a team. Of

course, you never know what Hong Kong or NY are up to at the moment. But if each one is doing his homework assignment, the company will profit. The ›big deals‹ are not only transacted in London, they are brought off on a global platform. For this purpose we have international phone and video conferences.

The office tower of HSBC on Canary Wharf

Kathy, waitress at a huge coffeehouse chain

- What do you notice about the London bankers?

Ok, up to 7 out of 10 of our customers in this store work in the financial industry. Respectively, in our café one has to pay a high price, for a high quality. Most suit wearing professionals don't mind the prices, however, they don't even pay attention to that! They just hand me their business credit card … Sometimes they even meet customers here or hold a meeting.

- What kind of influence does the financial centre have on the City itself?

It definitely pushes the price level. In this place, some goods are grossly overpriced compared to other cities or countries. But the terrific office towers decorate the city, and I really like that.

- What kind of influence does the financial centre have on the whole of London?
Next to the high prices there are some positive effects. The office buildings attract visitors from all over the world, for example, a fact that also helps our economy. Also the means of transportation by taxicab or metro tube are way more perfected – in order to get bankers to their meetings on a fast track.

A wealthy area in the Fulham district

Christopher Cloke-Browne, managing partner of an investment company

- Mr Cloke-Browne, is there anything you don't like about the City?

America is much more open-minded than London: I don't like that about London. Besides, it rains too often here [laughs].

For me, New York is much more a place for finance than London. In the past it showed that New York has a drift to make greater profit and close better deals. This may not come across to those who are not involved in the financial industry; but for us professionals it is a fact.

- What does money mean to you?

Money is a reference for your success demonstrating how well off you are. This forms a ranking system. So, the one who has the most money is on top of the list. The unfair distribution of wealth, the 99% : 1% statistics, emerges in the wake of the exponential growth of the compound interest.

A recreation area within the City, near Bishopsgate

Theo, working in the CSR [Corporate Social Responsibility] for a large financial institution

- What makes London outstanding as a financial location?

Evidently, its size! The London financial industry is a massive and powerful part of London's economy, as well as having a strong history and legacy. The fortunate time zone in between the Americas and Asia sweetens this matter.

- What do you like about London as a financial centre?

I really like the high level of innovation in London, and due to its nature as a major hub, the consequent influence that this innovation can have on the industry. This can be applicable to complicated structures, but also to new and socially powerful financial mechanisms such as social impact bonds which were developed in London and have a large international potential. Time and again there are new models we are working with. These models are hard to explain to outsiders, however.

- What would London be without its City?
It would just be another Paris: it would be less competitive and less innovative.

- Is there anything that could cause a crisis in the City?
Internally: a range of internal scandals, like the LIBOR trading scandal we have recently witnessed; or a vast trading loss of a major bank. Externally: new legal enactments could become a major problem for the City and its current business model.

- Which three terms can describe the City?
Good question! Flash, brash, big, I should say. You could also say: pretentious, presumptuous, potent.

▪ What happens behind these glass fronts? What kind of secrets are hidden?
A whole lot is happening behind the facades of financial institutions … Yet these things generally will not appear in public for various reasons …

The glass front of BNP Paribas

Mr Hart, Occupy-supporter

- What would London be without its City?
London would be a different city. Without the financial centre all the amazing buildings like ›The Shard‹ or ›The Gherkin‹ would be unnecessary and left London a less interesting place. Seen also from a social and of course from an economical point of view, London would change. You can sense it: the City has great influence on London.

- How would you react, if the forth empty plinth on Trafalgar Square had a banker's statue on top?
I'd rather have an Occupy-member on top of the fourth plinth. Namely we better comply with the Londoners than the financial employees; as you can also realise in the sad truth about the 99% : 1% statistics.[16]

---

[16] The unfair spread of wealth.

- Are violent demonstrations necessary?

I am absolutely against violent actions. And Occupy London just the same, although many people don't know that at all.

- How would you react if in the Tube a banker in front of you loudly bragged about his million-bonus?

Good question! I normally don't simply address strangers. But if I was provoked by a banker loudly speaking about his recent 2 million pound bonus, I would respond.

Homeless person close to Hyde Park

Gio, director of an investment fund

- What would London represent without its City?

It would still be the capital of Great Britain [laughs]. No, but it would still remain an important city with lots of energy and attract ambitious people.

- What is the impact of the financial centre on the town of London?

Prices are higher than in other major cities, since a lot of rich people live here in London, a fact that might correlate with the financial industry … Since the finance industry is a very international industry, it contributes to make London a very cosmopolitan city.

- What do you like about the City?

As I mentioned: those people from all over the world. I like the different cultures which globally link London, so to speak, with the whole world.

- What is it you don't like about the City of London?

The financial centre is simply too vast and thus influences the whole town too much. If the financial industry is struck by hard times, there will be negative consequences for the whole town.

- What is it that makes London singular as a financial centre?

We benefit enormously from the times zones allowing for live-trade with New York and Asia. In addition, we speak the universal language. Therefore, we can interact and deal without any problem with NY or Asia.

- Why is the number of women in the financial industry so low?

This is right now changing! On the entry-level the gender percentage is 50/50. In the higher positions the male part still dominates. But I'm very certain this will be different within the next 20 years.

- Has it always been your dream to work in the financial sector?

No, not at all. I was studying Economics in New York and originally I intended to pursue an academic career. But I got to know people working in the financial industry in the 1980s when new financial products were being created and got very interested in this field.

Stock exchange prices at the Reuters Building at night

Joris Luyendijk, non-fiction author and foreign correspondent, currently at ›The Guardian‹

- What impact does the financial centre have on London?

Most talented people in Great Britain go to London to work in the financial sector, though the crisis is slowly changing this somewhat. Nonetheless this brain drain towards the center creates an enormous gap between London and the rest of the Kingdom, since just in London they have the money, and roughly speaking, only there is any economic growth.

- What would London be without its City?

I'd compare it then with Paris or Bucharest. It would still be a superior city as to wealth and architecture, but not as ground-breaking and attractive to rich people.

▪ Why is the number of women in the financial business so small?
By now it is 50:50. The marketing and the human resources department are somewhat rather attractive for women. Investment banking takes a long wind and a lot of energy with its long working hours and high working pressure. This doesn't seem suitable for many women in the long run, especially after they have kids.

›The Guardian‹ building from the outside

Otto Dixx, investment professional at a real estate fund

- What do you like about the City of London?

The internationality, and that the population is from all kinds of countries and cultures. The night life in London also deserves recommendation.

- Do you dislike anything about the City of London?

Quite a lot! The weather, the stress, the bankers, and that it isn't Paris [laughs].

- What kind of influence does the financial centre have on the urban area?

Good question! Quite obviously, the financial centre is pushing the price level in London, making things harder for those who don't make the big bucks. In the West we've got a monoculture, about 90% are rich. This includes the municipal districts Chelsea, Mayfair, or Notting Hill. Some parts of London are little influenced by the financial centre, like the North or the East. I like it there better than in the West or in the centre.

- Why is the number of women so low in the financial world?

Women are less enthusiastic about watching excel spreadsheets all day, which I personally can well relate to. Men are eager to achieve prestige and esteem with a job in the financial sector; at least this is how it used to be.

- What is your personal aim for the future?

Good question, which I don't have an answer for. Did I know a future aim, I presumably wouldn't work in this trade any longer.

A banker during his lunch break, Bishopsgate district

Swen Lorenz, private investor, entrepreneur, advisor

▪ What makes London out-standing as a financial metropolis?
London has the perfect location to deal with Wall Street and Asia on the same day. The time zones are a big advantage for us here. Since it geographically lies in the middle between NY and Asia, London downright acts

as a centre. And because everyone here speaks English and English happens to be the standard language for worldwide deals, we don't face any troubles understanding our international partners. Also the English financial laws: they are the basis on which many international deals and treaties are grounded.

The lounge of one of the numerous tower buildings in the City

Mr Scooter, investment manager at a hedge fund

- What would London be like without the City?

London has been renowned as a world trading centre since the 19th century. So it would still be focussed on commerce, national and international, even without a booming financial sector. The financial centre however, the City, is probably the natural evolution of an Empire, where trading has become virtual as much as physical.

- What, in your opinion, will change in the financial industry and especially in London? What would you change?

The London financial world is being more and more regulated. The barriers for the entry-level will be higher than before. Banks and funds will have to fulfil more requirements to be ranked as an official company. This, in my view, will consequently lead to less competition and even higher prices. I personally would change little.

- How does a regular business day look like?
At 6:30 I'll get up and ride my motor scooter to work. I will work there from 8 a.m. till 8 in the evening. In between, I have some time for a short workout in the gym or a round of golf simulator. Every other week I fly to Switzerland or to Italy for work. I can't complain.

- Do you like to work right here? Which other place could also attract you?
I love working here and would only move from here if I could take my friends and family with me. In that case, Sydney would be an interesting place for me.

Almost omnipresent: ›The Shard‹

Why London works as a financial centre

One third of the $4.7 trillion daily worldwide foreign exchange trading streams through London's financial centre, according to a report by the Bank of International Settlements [BIS][17]: in foreign exchange trading London is leading worldwide. And the London Stock Exchange gets the third place of the global equity trading after New York and Tokyo. What advantages has London that other cities lack? Why is the world's biggest finance centre just in London?

London benefits enormously from its geographical location in-between the eastern and western time zones; in the morning LSE opening hours overlap and two hours with

---

[17] http://countingpips.com/fx/2011/08/8-largest-forex-trading-centers-in-the-world/

Hong Kong SEHK and Singapore SGX, and in the afternoon four hours with NYSE. Before the Asian market is closing, the market in London opens, and before the London markets is closing, Wall Street opens its lines.

But Frankfurt is only one hour ahead of London, so why is Frankfurt not as big a financial centre? It is the language. English is the global universal language with about 1.5 billion native or second language speakers, being the official and link language in 80 of the currently 194 nations of earth. Therefore London's finance institutions can negotiate with American companies and banks on the same level as well as with Australian, Canadian, Indian, South African …

Ben, founder of a non-profit organization, answered the question why he located his company domicile in London: »London is the centre of attention.« How did it become this centre of attention? Many of my interviewees appealed to London's history, London counted as a finance centre since the 16th century; and the City probably is the true heir of the British Empire …

Besides, the laws of Great Britain are globally oriented. »You can do in London what is illegal in New York«, said Michael Gold, an Occupy activist. Otto Dixx, an investment professional of a Real-Estate fund, spoke of the ›immigration of banks‹, resulting in an accumulation effect. If one bank locates a branch in the city, has success and creates a stir, other banks will follow readily, and another one, and another one … It's a bit like group pressure.

Three words depicting London's financial centre

… there are none. My interview partners found more, and often different terms to grasp the City shorthand. A pattern was formed however: ›innovative‹ was found to be the most frequently used term by the interviewees who work in the Financial Sector. ›Corrupt‹ was often said from Occupy. ›Quick and big‹ was the description used by neutral people whom do not belong in the Financial Sector.

The most exciting word used for the London Financial Sector was: ›Frankenstein.‹ This came from Brett Scott. He suggested that one can love or hate the Finance Sector, just as one can love or hate Frankenstein. So either the city profits as being a financial center, or it is being ruined by it.

The Occupiers found further critical words, an example being ›The City of Scandal‹. Michael Gold, a supporter of Occupy, indicated his opinion with these three words: ›bunch of crooks.‹ This was the harshest statement found from all of my interviewees.

Dave Dewhurst called it »self-deluding, mostly evil« and whilst grinning added: »Oh, I know these sound like four words, but the financial centre doesn't deserve merely three!« Clive Menzies, an Ex-banker and Funds Manager currently working for Occupy, describes the City as »mighty, intelligent and corrupt.«

So here appears to be one thankful Ex-Banker after all, as no other Occupy supporters had described the city to be intelligent. To the contrary. Occupy supporters insist they understood more about the economy and the workplace compared with those who actually work in the Financial Sector. There anyone is too constrained with one's knowledge and knew the score only in one's specific range.

»These untalented Oxbridge guys,« was an Occupy-phrase used to describe the characteristics finance-businessmen. ›Oxbridge‹ being a combination of the Universities Oxford and Cambridge. These are the two universities from which many large banks or funds often recruit, since the best of the best experts study at these most prestigious universities.

›Focused,‹ ›efficient,‹ ›powerful,‹ ›exclusive‹ are the descriptive words most used by my interview partners, I have noticed.

Focused, for the bottom line only allows for one option: to win. Efficient and not simply effective: for the desired effect is not simply obtained somehow, but rather with the most professional method. In the Financial Sector there appears to be a number of intelligent workers, always finding newer, faster ways to their goals, though that often turns the scale against others.

Powerful and competitive: for the majority of the Financial Sector is a strong battle, whereby the winner is being looked for. »Winners don't make excuses when the other side plays the game.«[18] So everyone looks for the most proficient method to be better than all the everyone else …

Exclusive: as London is THE largest financial center in the world and as such no place else can mimic it. The combination of the volumes most forex trading course, the most ideal location between the time zones of the earth, the world language, and the presence of the biggest and most well-known financial service providers is found nowhere else, currently.

---

[18] Harvey Specter, US-TV-series ›Suits‹

London without its financial industry?

What would London be without its financial centre? This question made a lot of my interviewers wonder, they had to think about it a minute before they could find an answer. This means to me in return that for Londoners London might not be imaginable without the City at all.

»A lot of the people I know think the economy would have to suffer,« says Ben from Positive Money[19]. But despite what one could think, so Ben, the main employer in London is not the finance industry, but the restaurants, bars and hotels that come with it. So probably the employment rate wouldn't have to suffer as badly as many may guess. On the other hand, the bars and restaurants themselves depend partly on the financial business

---

[19] see: www.positivemoney.org.uk

and the frequent consumption of its tradesmen. The restaurants serve them as neutral meeting spot with their clients – it is all a big part of an internal value chain. Part of the food suppliers appears to be a part of the financial sector infrastructure, and some waitress couldn't survive in London without the generous tips of its money businesspeople – the branches are tightly connected and one couldn't be without the other. Corresponding to this the answers to the question were as different as the people asked. One half told me, London would be poorer, also with regard to the City's striking architecture.

London would still be London even without the finance industry, others claimed. There were enough big-scale, prospering

and thriving branches in England's capital: culture could prosper and bring the town to life with art, music, fashion and film works. One of the arts would take the financial industry's lead and supply the metropolis with that certain buzz. Certainly: London would remain a cosmopolitan spot for people from all of the world's 200 nations. No other city holds an image more international to its name than London. Since 2001, more than 1 million people migrated to the capital of England [since 2004, approximately 650.000].[20]

Parade of national flags above Regent Street

---

[20] ONS, Office for National Statistics [http://www.ons.gov.uk/]

Like the financial industry: other branches work globally, too, and almost everyone might find chances to get involved. For 10 years, Mike Ross has been in charge of the Strategic Equity Transactions Group in a major bank of London. Three sectors are main source of London's appealing effect, so he says: this town is held up as an integral metropolis by financial, cultural and international aspects equally. If one of the three columns shattered, the remaining two branches were too dominant and the balance would be ruined. What seemed to be very important to most of my respondents was the fact that especially the financial district has given rise to all of the city's history and has a strong historical background. Since then, one should not underestimate the huge influence the City has on the remaining parts of London, for better or for worse.

»As the City impacts the whole of London too much, its crashing would have disastrous consequences for London itself,« Mr Hart answered, some of whose friends were imprisoned during the time I had my interview with him. They had put up a banner on Tower Bridge saying »climate change – our next challenge,« so they got arrested by police officers due to suspicion of criminal property damage. Actually, I was supposed to have a meeting with one of his friends, but ten minutes before it was to start, I received a text message saying »Sorry, I'm in jail. No meeting today.« My appreciating first thought on that was »Wow, how appropriate, really a ›stereotype‹ occupier!«

I myself cannot imagine a London without the City. In any case, global trade and finance businesses will very probably exist, by whatever means. And no other central European city would be an adequate replacement to London; it just worked almost frictionless as a major financial spot for hundreds of years so far.

What would London look like without The Gherkin or Lloyd's? To a certain extent, bankers and tradesmen define the picture of London, and with their designer suits, they suddenly seem to design the city's image itself. Without banking business people, this part of London's image would crumble, that of the titivated made-to-measure suit wearing businessmen. That would be as much a loss to London's charm like the vanishing of the bearskins of the Scots Guards in front of Buckingham Palace …

The J.P. Morgan high-rise – everything from impressive to depressive?

What will change?

»More regulations.« »Regulate the market and break its monopoly.« »Just regulate this goddamn system!«

These or similar reactions was what I got when I asked what will change in the financial industry. Depending on the attitude, some voices sounded full of regret, some more bittersweet and some angry.

Mr France, from a banking association in London, wondered why I posed this question in future tense. Banks are just now trying hard to bring their financial products closer to their clients and put easy information across. The biggest goal is not to let things happen again that lead to the last crisis. For that matter, banks are looking for new ways to organise their companies in a firmer and more stable structure. What is supposed to change or to reshape the system, is already changing at present.

On a large scale, expansive decisions are being made at the biggest financial center of the world. Businessmen and traders themselves call their deals ›bets‹, although they refrain to refer to what they do as ›bet‹ in public. A supporter of the Occupy movement described London as »City of scandal. Everyone wants to win, but that just won't work.« Trading losses up to billions frequently occur[21]. Legitimately, occupiers are alarmed by that fact and grow truly grim: as long as tax-payers have to settle these debts …

Banks owning the bets on rising and dropping shares usually have installed safety systems as well as backups in their data bases and

---

[21] http://www.business-standard.com/article/international/ex-credit-suisse-trader-arrested-in-london-in-trading-scandal-112092700102_1.html

host systems. Despite that, there are always individuals who are able to get past these barriers, so they can move and work out of the regulated range. Like in the scandal of LIBOR recently[22]. LIBOR [London Interbank Offered Rate] is a certain rate of interest of the BBA, which queries banks about the interest rates at which they lend money to each other. Highest and lowest rates get eliminated to prevent manipulation. Now, some big banks are being accused of having rigged the rates to their own advantages, to benefit from lower rates of interest. »So corrupt is only the City of London and the Italian Mafia,« Daniel O'Crisis reckoned, another supporter of the Occupy movement.

»More regulations, stricter laws and less risky bets – well okay, that will unfortunately

---

[22] http://www.zeit.de/wirtschaft/2012-08/libor-zinsen-manipulation-london

affect our wages,« Otto Dixx regrets.[23] »That's how the financial merchants will react to those laws that will make it harder for them to gain profit: of course they will cut the salaries of their workers. There will simply be more laws that have to be strictly adhered to, which actually can be evaded like before,« he added. »Some people will always find holes in the system and then cause a stir.« Personally, he would tax the profits of banks and hedge funds much higher, to change the distribution of power.

This division of power is also what Tobias mentioned, an investment banker of Lloyd's Building. About the unequal dispersion of capital: the richest 1 percent of the world's population owns approximately 99% of all existing wealth and fortune. That means that 99% are sharing the rest – merely 1% of all the

---

[23] Actually, he literally said: »Harder rules, more regulations and more bullshit …«

capital! Many workmen and employees don't know about this fact. The question »How many billionaires are here on earth?« would get you the most fantastic guesses. According to Forbes, there are only around 1300 billionaires in the world, among them 35 from the UK. Melanie Fletcher from Occupy London pointed out: the goal of the Occupy movement is exactly to get rid of these imbalances and to establish a fairer redistribution of money for the whole of the population. »The one-percent-change,« is what she calls it.

My impression after four weeks of interviews and observations in the City: the system keeps mum; the City seems staunch, the legislative authorities provide to maintain the present status the well-proven methods. Nonetheless, the monetary system will develop. Above all, I can't believe people will continue to be so cagey about one single business in a transparent enlightened future. Any London mechanic would have been keen on his name appearing in a book about London mechanics, same for producers of consumer goods, for artists, for actors … But not so for London bankers: not one single one would ever want his name to appear in a book about London bankers.[24] That I would have anticipated for weapon dealers or secret agents …

So I wonder most »What is it that absolutely has to be kept secret?«[25] Will it do good for a business branch in the long run, to seal itself off of the public? Of course, there is the matter of data protection. But how does an enterprise hope to persist in total secretiveness, while it might need the backup and understanding of the general public which is strongly influenced by it? Why not make things public where the public is concerned? Might finance business evolve from the black-

---

[24] Ok, Occupy activists were precautious, too: no photos, not even of the tent camps.

[25] Ok, evaded taxes, money-laundering …?

box-business it seemed to be to a more transparent, sustainable value-gaining …? There might be more modern thinking bankers to come … I would love to work in the finance business, as it keeps developing.

Sit-down-prohibiting-devices around a bank building

Non-profit-organisations at London's financial districts

Surprisingly, there is a great number of non-profit organisations in London that have to deal with the financial industry, right next to banks or hedge funds.

Lily Lapenna has founded MyBnk, for example. »MyBnk is a charity which delivers financial and enterprise education directly to schools and youth organisations.«[26] MyBnk-employees teach at schools and instruct students how to deal with their own money. In 2010, Mrs Lapenna received a fellowship-programme at Ashoka, a great international non-profit organisation supporting social enterprises.

---

[26] http://mybnk.org/about/what-is-mybnk/

Our first interview appointment had to be postponed, since Mrs Lapenna was asked to Harvard at short notice and had to meet with potential investors in Silicon Valley afterwards.

Her answers at our interview then showed that she looks upon the City and finance in general as ›outdated‹, as ›bygone‹! It is her aim to enable young people access to education, especially concerning financial matters. »Finance – this industry is the past« she says. »It's more important for everyone to be able to manage his own money and not to trust these Cityboys«, thus one of her statements. In my opinion, MyBnk is a valuable organisation and should be continued and extended in any case; maybe they can even succeed on an international level. The interest of investors could already be wakened, two of whom I personally could interview [they did not want to appear by name, however].

Positivemoney[27], founded by Ben Dyson, is another non-profit organisation. Their goal: revealing the connections between our present finance- and banking system and the largest social, economic and the most sustaining tasks. Ben Dyson wants to reform the financial system to weaken the power of high finance and large scale banking to create money without let or hindrance. This should not be possible for any large scale bank. It should be possible, however, in a transparent and accountable mode, traceable by anyone.

Bertrand Beghin is the founder of Numbers4Good. »Numbers4Good is a pioneering financial organisation with a conscience. We create financial solutions that allow organisations to fund social and environmental projects as well as connect investors with opportunities for sustainable financial and social

---

[27] http://www.positivemoney.org/

returns,«[28] quoting the project's philosophy.

Quite a number of ex-bankers I was able to meet and also people who were formerly otherwise engaged in the financial system have switched to the social side. Some of these ex-financiers have become sceptical towards the lack of scruple in some places within the financial world and now counteract with social engagement. There is a strong upward trend towards developing new models or persistent systems that will work for the future and are sustainable. It is the clear aim to avoid crises or totally abolish them.

Above, only a few examples of non-profit organisations have been mentioned. If you google »non-profit organisations London finance«, you'll get about 125,000,000 results; this also shows the increasing significance of the movement.

---

[28] http://www.numbers4good.com/

I got the impression that those characteristically financial start-ups are on the rise, which are involved with the non-profit sphere. In order to be effective for the future, sustainability is getting more and more important in finance [the crises of 2002 and 2008 revealed what can happen and which far-reaching consequences can evolve]. Why? Maybe simply, because sustainability makes sense.

With upcoming socially compatible financial organisations, the world of finance will change. As investors now invest into sustainable and future-bound start-ups, and not any more into huge and risky investment banks featuring anti-social assets and projects, the number of six-digit bonus payments will also decrease – a fact that will delight most Londoners who are afflicted with the gap between the rich and the poor. Social factors might come to light more in the City within the next future.

What I noticed

After four weeks in London's districts like ›The City‹ or ›Canary Wharf‹, you notice a lot of details and also big things which tourists wouldn't implicitly realise.

In the City you first wade through a sea of suits, shirts and ties. Interestingly, you'll only see that on four days a week. Why so? On so-called »Dress Down Friday«, Cityboys grant their ties a miss to celebrate with girlfriends or fellows right after their working hours.

But there are also differing dress codes within almost every department of the finance industry during the week, Joris Luyendijk revealed to me. Mr Luyendijk is a journalist at ›The Guardian‹ who keeps a banking blog in which he interviews finance people about the financial Centre of London [just like me, but full time …][29].

Bankers wear suits. But these suits differ in colour or accessory depending on the departments they work for. Employees from the corporate-finance departments wear bails on their shoes. In the IT department, almost no one wears a suit. Also hedge fund managers actually only wear suits when they meet with clients.

But in every department, rookies should buy the most expensive watch which they can afford. Showing that they are ready to spend money for clothing and accessories, they also exhibit their motivation to work there long term [at least long enough to earn ›back‹ the money for the watch].

Before I met with Tobias in the Lloyd's Building, he sent me a facebook message saying: »Please dress quite smartly, no jeans!

---

[29] http://www.guardian.co.uk/commentisfree/joris-luyendijk-banking-blog

Otherwise they will not allow you in – old fashion rules …«

The Lloyd's Building, built between 1978 and 1986, was innovate in having its services such as lifts and water pipes on the outside [designed by Richard Rogers]

Mr Luyendijk, who gave me an understanding of the dress codes and the structure of banks and funds, asked me at the end of our conversation how I had managed to get this appointment with him anyway! »That was a long chain of coincidences …« was my right answer. The chain included five people, each one recommended me to one of their business friends or colleagues, almost like a snowball system. This way, I could experience the density of the expertise in the City within my own project; if anyone is convinced enough of an idea in the City, he won't have troubles finding others willing to participate.

On a Saturday evening, I met up with a banker and his female colleagues. He works in a bank's M&A department [mergers and acquisitions].

I asked him in passing, if he could tell me an exciting detail, which no other interviewee could have told me. He mentioned casually the takeover bid of Rhön-Klinikum by Fresenius, he said it will be failing. I was a little bit shocked when he told me that! This was not what I really expected, I rather questioned him on something that only finance people inside the industry could be conspicuous about.

The meeting with my interview partner was held on Saturday, the 1st of September 2012. Next Monday morning, the share of Rhön lost 20% in value. He had precisely forecasted this. The M&A-employee emphasised his anonymity, as he could get fired. I'm not allowed to even mention his first name in this book, not even in the acknowledgements [so no use to type every name in linkedIn trying to find a banker who works in an M&A department in London's finance centre …].

Surely I already had signed the compliance contract right at the reception on arrival for the interview, saying I was forbidden to expose any of the information I witnessed here prematurely. Of course I told not a single soul about any inside information. But that I could gain knowledge of monetary benefits quite easily, by simply perking up my ears in London's City, I realized how hard it must be not to play off one's advance of knowledge for one's own benefit.

Wearing a suit gets uncomfortable in summer outside of air-conditioned buildings. But how elaborate these finance high-rise buildings are built, it's so well-conceived, double-skin facade to keep things breezy on demand! Sun rays will hardly touch the streets, keeping it nice and cool down there. During my 30 days in London last summer, it only rained 3-4 hours – not per day, but altogether! At the beginning of the trip, I kept asking myself if I was in the right London at all [my atlas shows at least four other cities called London, some in Canada and the US]. The capital of the United Kingdom is known as a rainy foggy city; surprisingly though, the thermometer showed always around 27° at blue skies.

Expectedly, you can see many business people in the street with smartphones. Either they phone or type on it. By listening randomly to their conversations, I noticed it isn't always about their work, but rather what to do after-hours; whereas work and leisure-time flow into each other.

Dennis Lavine, a trader of a major investment bank, once whipped out his iPhone during our interview; the phone was protected by an imprinted one-dollar bill cover. This telephone conversation lasted 20 seconds and was to settle the question if either he or his colleague was invite the client to the pub.

You soon notice the cleanness in the City. Due to the many cleaners, the finance centre keeps being ›clean‹ … You see them on every corner of the glass facades. Also the frontage of ›The Gherkin‹ is constantly cleaned by a specialist team of nine men [by letting gondolas down on ropes; it takes them nearly ten days to complete, then they start over …].

This results in crass pictures: the cleaners with their neon vests between the suited and FT-carrying Cityboys.

White vests, clean streets … But what if you need a dustbin to dispose your rubbish? Then you notice a weirdness in the tube stations: there aren't any dustbins to dispose your rubbish! Scarcely a little transparent plastic bag. I asked myself: why? And someone taught me: on safety grounds. At the 7th of July 2005, four bombs exploded in London, three of them in the underground and one in a red double-decker bus. Well, now no one can hide bombs easily anymore in a plastic bag.

Especially during the Olympics, it was important that no bombs explode. As I met with Bertrand Beghin in a little café near Oxford Street. When a customer beside us suddenly left the café without his bag, Bertrand got immediately uneasy. At first, I didn't understand why, as I had not noticed the bag consciously as my London interviewee. It looked similar to the following picture, a forsaken bag in a café house:

Bertrand asked the waitress right away if he could check the bag, at which she responded: »No, he was here yesterday as well. Maybe he just calls someone. At least that's what the customer told me yesterday.« »I don't care what that guy told you: he could tell you anything!«, Bertrand Beghin replied in an angry voice. I also became worried; we continued the interview, but my interview partner seemed a bit distracted. After 10 minutes, the owner of the bag returned. Bertrand was wild about him and attacked him verbally. »In London, people don't like it when someone leaves the room without his bag.« Right. During the Olympics, the safety situation is fussier than usual and the Londoners are especially sensitive to someone who arouses suspicion …

Often I met other respondents of the finance industry in cafés or small bars as well. Every single one of them, yes, every single one invited me to a drink or snack. This was sometime getting somewhat uncomfortable for me, so I wanted to invite my next interview partner. But he just laughed and said: »My employer pays that for us, so don't worry«, and pulled out his corporate card.

An interesting fact for me was also: each pedestrian I addressed, knew what I was talking about and what I meant by the finance centre. I didn't take this as a matter of course. For example, does everybody in Karlsruhe know the Federal Constitutional Court, Germany's highest court, has its domicile in Karlsruhe? I don't think so, I know some people from Karlsruhe who can't connect their city with the ›City of law‹. Well, a few interviewees asked me from which German city I come from. »Karlsruhe, it's nearby Frankfurt«, was my answer, as ›Mainhatten‹ should be known to every business man in London. A common response was: »Ah, yes I know Karlsruhe. We say, it's the City of Law!«

The last Monday in August is a public holiday in Great Britain, the so-called ›bank holiday‹. I couldn't believe it first there is a bank holiday! No other country offers such a holiday. In Germany there is not even an autocar holiday, for example. If England instituted a special bank holiday, the finance industry has to have a remarkable position.

This Monday, the City was almost completely empty, I didn't spot any suit wearing City-workers, as many of them used this long weekend to travel to Switzerland or Italy for hiking; or to their families, like they told me.

Many interviewees of the finance industry stated they even use short weekends to travel. Popular destinations are the Alps, the Côte d'Azur or their countries of origin. »I need this to compensate the enormous pressure at work,« was one of the most common explanations; fair enough, with 70-80 working hours per week. Mr Scooter could literally recite the entire German Airport announcements, although he might not understand a single syllable of it. »Sehr geehrte Damen und Herren, für den Weiterflug nach Frankfurt am Main begeben Sie sich bitte zu Gate Nr. 21.« He flies away every other weekend.

Millions of pigeons seem to find London an attractive destination! Everywhere – even in the City of London, with its skyscraper canyons actually being kind of hostile to birds, ›birdphobic‹. Conspicuously many pigeons are hurt, they only have one leg or only three toes left instead of four.

Did this pigeon fall victim to a stressed Cityboy? Cityboys often get into a fret with these birds and some of them kick at them, what could account for some of the pigeons' injuries. One business man I heard shouting »F*** off!« as he waggled his arm towards a feral pigeon blocking a bench he wanted to use to keep on telephoning and eating on the side. Why so aggressive against these birds of peace? Well, a single fecal drop ruins the entire £1000 suit, and you'd have to change it right away.

At the beginning, the greeting rituals in England somewhat confused me. British ask »Hi, how are you?«, but don't expect any answer, rather get to the point instantly. At first, I kept responding »I'm good, thanks. How are you?« But after earning puzzled glances, I stopped doing that. Altogether, I could fit into the language very quickly and understood almost all sentences after the third or fourth interview. I have noticed that nearly all Occupy members used a very sublime sophisticated language which was at first harder to understand than the English of the bankers. The other interviewees were easier to understand; might they have aligned their vocabulary to my ›nonnative speaker English‹?

The organisation in this city, in the offices and in people's minds surprised me in a positive way. Early in September there was a big festival at Piccadilly Circus called ›Piccadilly Circus Circus‹. At the show's finale, the acrobats blew more than 1.5 tons of feathers into the air. Piccadilly Circus equaled a snowscape. The very next morning on my way to the next interview, I stopped by there to see what had happened to the millions of feathers. Not a single feather in sight! That's what I call management and great organisation of a metropolis.

What I learned from London

You get a much better grasp of things and places if you actually go out to the place of interest and talk to the locals . By seeing things with one's own eyes you learn more than can ever be learned by just sitting at your desk. Now I imagine, while reading or studying in front of my terminal, how it would feel like if I could really be at the place I study about. What difference would it make!? That's why my journey occurred at the right moment, because I could find out the difference between sitting studies and actually experienceing field research.

Timing was also perfect, because my interview partners would probably not have spent one of their valuable hours with a much younger person and maybe not with a much older one either, who easily could have been a competitor.

Instead, they were frank with me, maybe as I had just attained full age, or because I am not a native speaker or because I came from a foreign country and was presumed to be a friendly and eager to learn UNESCO-scholar. I seemed harmless enough to them, so some would tell me things, which you would rather not tell your friends about. »They didn't see you coming,« someone commented. However, I never took advantage of insider information, I only used the kind openness of my interviewees as a jump start for stronger interview results – my interviewees must have seen that coming …

Arriving in London though I first had to revise my questionnaire [actually my preconceptions]: too often I used the word ›banker‹. »Some people get mad if you call them ›banker‹«, I heard several times. Alright, not everyone wearing a suit is a banker. But as my first interviewees – they were part of the financial sphere – firmly rejected the term, I realised: in the financial community ›bankers‹ are an exception.

Because fund managers, especially hedge funds managers are no ›bankers‹, they don't work in a bank: they definitely don't want to be approached as ›bankers‹. However, an umbrella term was hard to find; ›financier‹, ›business man‹ or ›finance people‹, some of my dialogue partners proposed. »I would say I'm an investment manager«, Mr Scooter said; he works at a hedge fund. In any case you definitely have to be careful with the term ›banker‹.

London appears like a city which is specifically built for financial institutions. I got to learn how everything needed by the financial industry is just there and right at hand: banks, law firms, funds, insurance companies, brokers, auditors, accountants, corporate consultants … You can think of it as a mind-map that became real, or a network. Much works through existing contacts. They route you on to the next one. Then add the giant infrastructure with the transport systems, the maintenance platoons, the security teams, the couriers and suppliers, restaurants and bars, the suit tailors, leisure-time entertainment and cultural establishments – this array of availabilities is perfectly targeted towards purposeful movements: the flow of traffic and the flow of money coalesce. Last not least the lawmakers add to the locational advantages, enforcing capital friendly laws like the COLL, the Financial Services Authority's [FSA] book of fund rules.

The financial district is indeed demarcated by its own district emblem; this district works by its own rules and has his own law[30], like a state within the town of London … The security system is remarkably perfected here. With half

---

[30] e.g. the king or queen of England must ask for permission before entering that territory [!]. There is also an independent police force.

a million security cameras on house walls, lamp poles, trees, tower buildings, the people working in the financial sector feel secure.[31]

After hanging a poster with some critical slogans in front of St. Paul's Cathedral, an Occupy activist I got to know received a penalty warning together with the pictures of a monitoring camera. The demand note said he was identified by a face detection software.

It's not all about counting money in the financial branch, as some might assume. Mr Scooter says, »compliance-stuff« costs him a lot of time. »If people were straightforward, I

---

[31] So in London there are two times more CCTV-cameras than in Beijing, which however is three times bigger than London … No city inhabitant on earth is more often electronically recorded than a Londoner, 300 times daily on average. [Source: »Revealed: Big Brother Britain has more CCTV cameras than China«; Tom Kelly, MailOnline, 11.8.2009]

would have more time for other things.« Instead, he needs hours to prepare compliance contracts; contracts in which associates and clients assure confidential treatment of all relevant data.

In films you see traders like this: they scream in phones and display weird gestures. When I visited a trading floor of a big US-bank in Canary Wharf, I was surprised how quiet and calm it was: »Today everything works through computers, not phones.« Computers are taking over and do the trading at the capital market. This so called high-frequency-trading came under criticism often lately. When the shares of a corporate giant suddenly lose 20% of their worth within seconds and there is not really a reason for it, high-frequency trading is often held responsible for it, and being questioned.

The appearance of business people in London really impressed me; their charisma, once you get closer to them. I truly had the impression: everyone not being a business person leaves more space to the business people, just as if they had a special aura, which should not be deranged; yes, I often saw normally dressed people dodging people in suits. Just as if they did not want to disturb the certainly important business of these suits beaming with power they left more space for them than they would leave for other normally dressed. Also on escalators many average mortals made room especially for suit wearing folks, so that those could pass faster without distraction.

The opinion of the opposition, from Occupy, is very insightful also. Their campaigns, their mission for a fair distribution of wealth, their sea of tents are just as impressive as the skyscrapers of the city. It almost seems as if the strength of the competitors mutually accounts for itself, as if the sheer power of the financial system within the city enforces a rhetorically just as highly cultured counterforce right next to itself.

What I also learned: real friends are important to have. Incarnate friends, whom you can shake hands with, who might invite you for a warm drink when it's getting cold outside and dark. Without the help of some friendly people, I would not have been able to bear up 4 weeks with my 600 Euros scholarship cash in my pocket in Europe's most expensive city …

A few numbers about my project

At a financial centre numbers count, numbers rule: and whoever shuns counting on numbers will hardly strike roots in the City. Gradually I realised, how I could grasp my own City-project better with numbers and how I could make it better understood by others.

So here are some figures: I arranged 44 appointments with interviewees. In 31 days I was able to interview 36 people; 9 women, 27 men. The share of women in the finance sector is small, therefore it was harder to find female interviewees. Thus, I more often just addressed my female interviewees in front of the main gates of high street banks or other financial institutions in order to schedule an interview on the spot, without a prefixed date.

How high exactly is the female and male proportion of the workpeople in the financial services industry, broken up numerically?

That seems to be unclear to the Londoners themselves. About 8 of 10 interviewees estimate the gender distribution to be 75:25, of 100 financial business people there would be 75 men and 25 women. Joris Luyendijk however assumes the rate to be 50:50, if one considers the finance sector altogether, but in the higher positions the female quota amounts to merely 15% yet.

Here is some statistics about my 44 interviewees:
16 came directly out of the financial sector,
8 came from non-profit-organizations,
7 from Occupy;
5 were ›neutral,‹ not involved in finance;
8 appointed interviews were cancelled[32].

---

[32] for instance as the interviewees were troubled by second thoughts concerning their contractual agreements of non-disclosure with their employers, or as they had suddenly

Only one third of my London interviewees originated from Great Britain [12 out of 36]. That fact, too, reveals the internationality of the city. At times it seemed a real challenge to even find a native of England! In the finance sector itself only 25% of my interviewees were English. Stephen Billion – he's of a major insurance group – told me, in his team of 25 there were only 2 native Englishmen. The predominant ›rest‹ stems from the USA, Canada, Germany, France, Ireland, Italy and Australia.

Out of 36 interviewees 12 gave me their business card, after I gave them mine; the others wanted, as I said, not to be mentioned by name. What helped me to get those interviewees at all: all of them were impressed by my preparations with my own business card – being a youngster to them – as well as with

---

rather left London over the crowded Olympic summer …

my book. Because the book you presently hold in your hands: I already had it printed before my trip, with almost identical cover – inside of course still empty, except for my questions. That way I could approach anybody showing them the book, saying: »I would like you to be in this book.« That got people interested.

And with my blank book I could take notes directly into the book's pages while interviewing. It must have looked to the interviewees as if that book was actually written in the same moment they were being interviewed. This blank book prompted some of the interviewees to at all support my project!

During my 4 week stay in London the British stock index ›FTSE 100,‹ called ›Footsie,‹ sank by 0,8%. That is from 5845,92 to 5794,80 index points.

In this month moreover, about 41 Billion Dollars were dealt in foreign exchange via

FOREX, the currency market [with a daily trading volume of 1,854 Billion Dollars]. With 37% of the world's daily volume, London is the largest financial centre on earth, concerning the trading with foreign currencies. 100% of my interviewees knew that, which impressed me. Even the half dozen ›neutrals,‹ randomly addressed pedestrians, knew about this information. That shows, that even London inhabitants not participating in the finance business know details on London's financial centre.

The distance traveled by me in London in August and September 2012: about 500.000 meters [500 kilometers], on a daily average of about 17 kilometers [by foot, Tube, bike, car, bus or boat …].

On an average day 3,2 million Londoners use the underground system, on weekdays it's almost 4 millions. Thus on the 30 days of my London time over 100 million times people were being transported by the Tube – had it been a ›normal‹ time; with the Olympics it must have been double rates, as with the prices …

Places, where I could experience the financial centre at work:
+ I saw 7-8 high-rise towers of funds- and investment-corporations and asset-management-companies from the inside [with other finance business people I spoke in the coffee bars or cafés they recommended, or even directly on the streets of the City];
+ I visited the Museum of the Bank of England;
+ the guided tour at the London Stock Exchange unfortunately got cancelled – in the meantime it does not take place at all anymore!
+ I could visit the Lloyd's Building for several hours;

+ on the trading floor of the City Group I could be present directly next to an authorized stock exchange trader – what a highlight!
+ I was finally not allowed to step on the trading floor of the metal exchange, like all ordinary mortals – despite hard negotiations;
+ I visited the headquarters of the British Bankers Association.

Conversation of two finance business men in the City next to Tower 42

The most memorable statements

»London is a playground for rich people.«
Tobias, Asset-Manager

»Business is about control. Mine is people business, so you need to know your partner, as you actually can't trust people with money.«
Mr Anonymous' reply to the question what counts when doing business

»It's the people who keep you in London, not the weather.«
James Almighty, Hedgefond-Manager

»Actually none of them, I want to stay healthy.«
Mike Group, Warrant Trader, if he wants to have a super power during his office hours

»On a good day, about 80%.«
Dennis Lavine, Head of M&A department at a British bank, to the question how many people work in his fund

»I had a job offer from a bank when I was 18, but my family said I should do something more respectfully.«
David Dewhurst, Occupy, if he would like to work in finance business

»A tradition I would do without.«
Mr Scooter, investment manager of a hedge fund, to the question why almost every finance fellow wears a suit

»There are too many Americans!«
Ben France, trader of a British investment bank, to the question what he dislikes at London's financial centre

»I'd be silly, if I say no.«
Mr Retire, spokesman of a bank network, if he disliked something in the City

»The finance business is the most sexist industry towards women!«
Robert Wilson, Ashoka, how he interprets the low female quota in the financial industry

»London reached a level of innovation, where it can get dangerous. So yes, as London can always become a bubble.«
A senior asset management executive, if he tends to work at another financial centre

What I found Interesting. Media list

»The Money Machine. How the City Works«; by Philip Coggan; fully revised and updated 6th edition, Penguin Books, London 2009

»How the City Really Works. The Definite Guide to Money and Investing in London's Square Mile«; by Alexander Davidson; 3rd edition, Kogan Page, London 2010

»Cityboy. Beer And Loathing In The Square Mile«; by Geraint Anderson; updated edition, first published in 2008, Headline Publishing Group, London 2008

»City of Scandal. Capital Capers«; by William Lee Adams and Kharunya Paramaguru; TIME-Magazin, July 23, 2012, pp. 18-21;

»Die globalen Hedgefonds-Domizile im Wettbewerb« [»The global hedge funds domiciles in contest. An overview over the legal framework of the most popular hedge funds domiciles«]; by Rolf Majcen; Vienna 2007

»Schäden in Milliardenhöhe« [Damage in the billions], DLF-Radio, Broadcast September 10, 2012

»Von Banken und Banden« [Of banks and bands], SWR2-Radio, ›Forum‹, Broadcast August 22, 2012

»Ratingagenturen. Einblicke in die Kapitalmacht der Gegenwart« [Rating agencies. Insights into the capital force of the present], SR2-Radio [Saarland Radio], ›Fragen an den Autor‹ [Questions to the author], Werner Rügemer; Broadcast August 12, 2012

»The City of London. Money and Power,«

BBC Documentation, http://www.youtube.com/watch?v=OD0lx9MKp7Q

»Der Preis des Geldes. Ein Thementag rund um Banken, Kredite und Macht« [»The Price of Money. A Theme-Day about Banks, Credits and Power«], 3sat-TV, Theme night, October 3, 2012

»Goldman Sachs – eine Bank lenkt die Welt« [»Goldman Sachs – a bank leads the world«], Arte-TV, Theme night, September 4, 2012

http://www.uk.reuters.com
http://www.bloomberg.com

http://countingpips.com/fx/2011/08/8-largest-forex-trading-centers-in-the-world/

Me in front of the Lloyd's Building, August 2012

Thank you! Acknowledgements

My sincere thanks for all your help and kindness goes to:

my parents;
Giovanni Pini, Giacomo Mergoni, Laura Pastondi;
Dirk Heß, Michael Gabel;
Danijel Jozic, Dagmar Baltes, Bernhard Bueb and all zis-helpers;
Sabina, Julia, Jana, Erik Orbach;
Ilana Taub, Rachel Sinha, Bertrand Beghin, Ben Dyson;
Brett Scott, Joris Luyendijk;
Christopher Cloke-Browne, Roz Drayer;
Lily Lapenna, Mike Mompi, Kathy Gromotka;
Julie Whittaker, Robert Wilson, Mark Cheng, Silvia Giovannoni;
Toby Rometsch
Jeremy Rogers

Alec McLaurin

Benôit Vanpoperinghe

Geraint Anderson

Hugo Griffiths

David Dewhurst, Clive Menzies, Michael Gold, Melanie Strickland, Peter Coville, Kevin Dowd, Geoff;

Brian Capon, Jacques Gauthe;

Stephen Millar

Swen Lorenz

Kathy

Claire Tappenden

Miriam De Morais

Josh Stevens

Isolde

Iraklis Nikolakakos

Tim Skelton-Smith

Christoph Warrack

Dennis Lavine

Daniel McGreggor

Claire Crooks

Mila

»Countries are different. They make different choices. We cannot harmonise everything.«
David Cameron